FEMININE MYSTIQUE IN THAT LONG SILENCE

DR. SHARMILA. S

ISBN 979-888606809-2

With deep love to my husband and my family for bearing with me and accepting my moods during the writing process

Contents

Acknowledgements

It fills me with immense gratitude to be able to accomplish the challenging task of completing this book through the blessings of the Almighty. The competition of this work would not have been possible without the support and encouragement of several people to whom I feel obliged and indebted. I am extremely grateful to my supervisor, **Dr.N. VijayaDurai**, M.A., M.Phil., PGDTE., Ph.D., Associate professor and Head, Department of English, Chikkaiah Naicker College, Erode for his solicited help, valuable mentorship. I thank him wholeheartedly for his fraternal love and care. His strive for betterment as well as the intense analysis of work that he does, inspires me to work harder. Sir has always encouraged me and has broadened my horizon through a constant discussion on the diverse aspects. Without his sincere help, encouragement, constructive criticism and invaluable advice, this book would have never been completed.

I like to express my most sincere thanks to **Dr. V. Balusamy**, Principal, Kongu Engineering College, Erode, who offered me an opportunity to do the publication in their esteemed institution. I whole heartedly thank him for his valuable support, encouragement and remarkable motivation throughout my academic career.

I extend my sincerest gratitude to the Dept. English and the entire teaching co- faculties of the department for their support and amicability throughout my tenure as an English professor. I am much obliged to **Dr.A.Robby Sebastian Clement**, Associate professor & Head and Department of English, Kongu Engineering College for his encouragement and support throughout the process.

Next, I am proud and happy to register my gratitude to **Dr.R.Palanivel**, Assistant professor of English, Annamalai University, Chidambaram, the versatile literary genius, for his loving, sage advice and especially for his generous, kind and patient reading of the drafts, scholarly suggestions for appropriacy and accuracy. As always, it was a pleasure conferring and sharing with him. I would be failing in my duty if I do not acknowledge **Dr. T.Magudeeswaran**, Librarian, Chikkaiah Naicker College, Erode, who has extended his unstinting support, provided many resources whenever I was in dire need. I would like to thank The Librarian and faculty members of Bishop Heber College, Tiruchirapalli and The University Librarian, National College, Tiruchirapalli, and for having readily helped me through the Libraries of their institution.

It is part of my feeling to express my heartfelt thanks to my parents and also my mother-in law and father-in law, always act as second parents of mine. Finally, my immense gratitude is to the person who encourages me, is always present with his support and love, and who unmindfully doing all things for the welfare of mine though I had almost estranged myself from my share of the household chores of late and happened to exercise inadvertent restraint on my usual cordiality, company and warmth and he is my life partner, **Mr.K.Kannan**, though I could never sufficiently thank my husband. Last but not the least I thank my child for having made me forget the exhaustion caused due to my work through his sweet talk and always has been asking, "Mom, what are you doing in computer all the time?"which indeed implied his disguised missing of my company during the weekends and other occasions.

Above all, once again I thank God Almighty for having blessed me with this life and a sensitive mind, and for making me deserve His showering of grace all these years as well as in all my endeavours inclusive of the present one.

Author Bio-note

Dr. S. SHARMILA M.A., M.Phil., B.Ed., TESOL an accomplished, student-centric, and an inquisitive English Professor, working as an Assistant professor of English, Kongu Engineering College, Erode, Tamil Nadu. She received her Ph.D. from Bharathiar University, Coimbatore. She is a skilled person in ELT and Literature. She regularly publishes articles and presents papers at various academic events. She has developed her skills in teaching English to adults, working as a trainer in Language academies. She has passionate in developing lesson plans and language games for both undergraduate and graduate students. Throughout her distinguished teaching career, she has been demonstrating an unwavering commitment to foster a deep appreciation for works of literature while honing with her communication, creativity, and motivational skills. Furthermore, her inherent passion for fostering collaborative and engaging educational environments has been successfully encouraged and developed productive, thoughtful, and accomplished English students. In addition, her 10 years of teaching experience and personal qualities have a solid educational foundation and a passion for education.

ONE
INTRODUCTION

Gender is a significant trait of a person's personality. It wields massive impact on our lives from the time of our birth, and we take steps according to its social and cultural aspects at crucial moments of our lives from beginning to end. Gender, part away from biological inequity, is a social and cultural structure of femininities and masculinities. As the theorist Simon de Beauvoir (1949) said all human beings are not born with natural tags of man or woman but it is society that formulates them either man or woman (118). Human beings create gender based categorization, hierarchies and classification among themselves.

Beginning of birth itself, children are treated on the basis of gender and they are given dissimilar treatments because of gender politics, and babies are not only clothed in different colors but are given different type of toys to maintain gendered partition. Gender split between male and female, shaped in different cultures and societies and manifests itself among the reactions of people. Some of the people are firmly against this chain of commands while others try to justify it.

In the same way, writers also bring fourth their responses in their writings. As this research concerns gender politics in Shashi Deshpande's novels, under study with the milieu of feminist literary theory in order to attain a better understanding of the hidden predicaments that are involved in gender representation. In order to verify gender characteristics and gender image, we need to make a distinction between sex and gender.

Sexual character and personality pass on to biological differences that classify someone as male or female; whilst gender pass on to the ideas, distinctiveness, characteristics and practices of masculine and feminine and is framed within a social framework. Oxford Advanced Learner's Dictionary delineates gender as "sexual classification; i.e sex, the male and female" (171). The hierarchical power associations and power relation between male and female are leading to the gender politics which promotes in marginalization and exploitation of women. This classification between genders is usually accepted as a natural phenomenon but is truly composed by society.

According to Reeves and Baden (2000), Gender politics is existed in patriarchal society to suppress women always.

"Gender relationships among the people are determined, in a culture, by a number of several operating authorities like family relations, legal system etc. These operating authorities are the reasons that are responsible for creating certain rules or regulations to control and manipulate social institutions. Even the history reveals the fact that women were marginalized and were not given equal rights to use their power to bring about change in the social sphere" (18).

Feminist Literary Theory is mainly related to the influence of gender on writings. It is often takes into an account of social discrimination and gender politics provides a critique to the patriarchal culture that is formulated to favor males. Feminists affirm that gender signifies nothing but the distinction between genders are constructed and imposed by the society and it leads to the gender politics.

Feminist theory affords a platform for the readers to come across the power constructions and power structures due to gender favoritism in a certain culture are reflected and challenged by the famous writers. Every major feminist critics, like Ellen Moers, Betty Friedan, Kate Millet, and Elaine Showalter, adopted a female related perspective focusing on literature by women and neglecting earlier exclusive emphasis on revealing sexist distortions, patriarchal stereotypes and gender politics.

Feminist literary critics exhibits in their criticism how often fictional images of women are a reflection of recognizable cultural stereotypes. These identifiable cultural stereotypical images include the woman such as morally depraved and dangerous seductress, perpetually helpless, self-sacrificing, innocent, inexperienced, and unworldly, etc. In view of the fact that, the way female characters were depicted had not much in common with the way feminist critics saw and experienced themselves. These characters were not real and natural but rather creations, put together but not necessarily by the writers who presented them to denote the culture they belong to serve. And exhibit the continued social and cultural domination of males. Particularly, in Indian English writing, Shashi Despande's novels depicts vivid picture of gender politics which makes women subjugated position and lower status because of gender supremacy.

Indian women novelists in English have dealt with the place and position of women in Indian society and their problems. Some women writers tried to tell the world about obstacles that the women faced and the disadvantages they suffered in an orthodox Hindu world. Indian women novelists aimed at portraying realistically about Indian women's sense of frustration, alienation and their quest for assertion of identity. Women writers in Indian English fiction have significantly contributed to the vitality, variety, humanity and artistic integrity.

Women have been the nodal point of several literary writings in post colonial India. Literature has reflected the changing life styles of the Indian women placed in the traditional, cultural backdrop of the Indian Society. It is also evident that the upsurge of political and social consciousness has encouraged women to shed the shackles of their placid stoicism. Consequently, women in Indian fiction have been treated both as symbols of retreat, personal regression and self-pity as well as symbols of growth, purity and development in the urban and rural milieu. They make frantic efforts to define themselves in a male dominated society. In their writings, post colonial Indian women writers have not only exhorted an exposition of the patriarchal ideologies and their oppressive tendencies toward feminist growth and expression but also have envisioned ways of counteracting those attitudes.

The Indian women novelists appear to be forced and contrived. Their neurotic characters too have been explained away in terms of feminism. Nayantara Sahgal's and Sashi Deshpande's novels are feminist concerns but only incidentally. Their protagonists are acutely aware of themselves as women. Women novelists have also shown their extraordinary caliber and immutable imprint in the realm of Indian fictions in English. They have shown their mettle in every field and in some respects, far better than the male novelists. The history of Indian women novelists in English generally begins with Toru Dutt. After the Second World War, Indian women novelists got a new track, a new vision.

Fiction by women writers provides searching insights and a great deal of human understanding. Shashi Deshpande is concerned with women's quest for self-exploration into female psyche and an understanding of the mysterious of life and the protagonists place in it. The vital insight that Deshpande brings to reader is that women should take their own responsibility for what they are and see how much they have contributed to their victimization

Women writers probe into human relationships, since the present problem is concerned with the mind and heart. The women writers particularly have shared the experiences of Indian women in general and transmuted into fictional form. Several highly talented women novelists including Kamala Markandaya, Anita Desai, Nayantara Sahghal, AttiHosain, Santha Rama Rau and Shashi Deshpande have enriched Indian fiction in English. They have written of Indian women, their conflicts and predicaments against the background of contemporary India. While doing so, they have analysed the socio-cultural modes and values that have given Indian women about their image and role towards them and the society.

The changing contexts have placed those women writers in unenviable position. Their chief involvement consists of their exploring the moral and psychic dilemmas and consequences of their women characters. They challenge and achieve a new harmony of relationship within themselves and their surroundings. Women bids good bye to her silence, anger and resentment. Women realize her self-worth and decide to give up the pre-fixed norms of the society. Rashmi Gaur observes: "The haunting riddle of the ultimate purpose of a woman's life within the family can be solved when she learns to assess her worth as an individual and shuns to be guided by pre-fixed norms about it". (179).

In India, both men and women writers have seen women in a typical relationships with men and they have noticed clear cut picture of gender politics prevailing in nook and corner of the patriarchal system of the society. Both sociologists and intellectual regard Indian society as a conventionally male-dominated one where individual rights are subordinated to group or social role expectations. Woman has often been a sufferer of male oppression and treated as a beast of burden. As a result, woman's individual self has no recognition and self-effacement is the only course left to her.

Indian woman has traditionally succumbed to this hierarchy, accepted her position and lived with it for ages. The novelists of the post independence period, who highlighted the causes of women, are Anita Desai, Shashi Deshapande and Arundhati Roy etc. Their main focus was on the undesirable dominance of men over women in the name of gender supremacy.

In the context of contemporary Indian writing in English, Shashi Deshpande is one of the most understated confident voices, who explore individual and universal predicaments through the female psyche. Characters are the most important aspect of her writing. Each of her fiction is special and offer food for thought on human relationship and emotions. She has been quietly writing for the last 30 years without fanfare and without ceremony.

In the early stage, novels are mostly dealt with the nationalistic feelings but after the 1950's the writers started to write their own problems and crises. Most of them in their eagerness tried to find new themes renounced the larger world in favour of the inner man and engaged themselves in a search for the essence of the human living. Shashi Deshpande is something different and she says that writers do not think consciously about style as critics do, for a writer the important thing is to find the voice. The story decides whether there should be single voice or multiple voices. In that *Long Silence* the single voice of Jaya may account for the tunnel vision but there is intensity.

Shashi Deshpande, a contemporary Indian writer, talks about her characters' self – analysis and self – understanding through and which they explore their self – identity and gender issues. She has written eight novels of which *That Long Silence* (1988) has a special mention. Shashi Deshpande's writing career began in earnest only in 1970, initially with the short stories, of which several volumes have been published. She is also the author of four children's book and novels. Shashi Deshpande was born in 1938 in Dharwad, Karnataka, India. She was the daughter of a renowned Kannada writer and Sanskrit scholar Adya Rangachar better known as Shriranya. At the age of fifteen, she went to Bombay, where she gained a degree in law. *The Dark Holds No Terrors (1980), If I Die Today (1982), Come up and Be Dead (1983) and Roots and Shadows* (1984).

She lives in Bangalore with her pathologist husband, and has recently completed her M.A. in English Literature. Deshpande's subjects are relatively of women's lives and the truths that lie behind their silence. She has appeared as a great literary force. She focuses on women's issues and she has women's perspective on the world. Deshpande is the best-known contemporary Indian women novelist. She is the recipient of Sahitya Academy award for her novel, That Long Silence. Deshpande's sincerity and ability in voicing the concerns of the urban educated middle-class holds a universal appeal. She believes that her work is having an impact on women's lives. She has been labeled a feminist because f her concern with women characters and the situations in which they find themselves. She believes that she simply writes about what she sees around her, and that her ideas follow naturally. Shashi Deshpande's female characters are ordinary middle class women, down to earth and face crisis of life silently and internally.

Deshpande is a prominent writer in the way she articulates human emotions, the fears and feelings experienced by humans, particularly by women. Women are considered to be an inferior gender. New novelists like Upamnya Chatterjee, Vikram Seth, Amitav Gosh and Shashi Deshpande in the eighties have published interesting novels on contemporary themes that make absorbing reading. As compared to many other Indian women writers of the twentieth century, she is much more vociferous in voicing her fears and concerns regarding the future of women in uncongenial surroundings. She is one of the leading writers of modern India. Her novels have been translated into seven European languages. Shashi Deshpande's novels, which describe the experience of the modern, educated, middle class Indian women, show similarities and contrasts to western feminists works.

Deshpande also enjoyed reading Dickens and Tolstoy. A picture is worth a thousand words. Nevertheless, each novel by Deshpande is worth a thousand pictures. Reading her books is like peeing into the corners of one's own mind. Identifying oneself in her characters, one does not sense lonely in the world anymore. Because she writes about the actuality of women lives and truths, that lie behind their silence. Even her works have also been translated into a number of Indian and foreign languages.

Most of her writings come out of her own intense and long suppressed feelings about what it is to be a woman in our society. Her writing comes out of consciousness of the conflict between her idea of herself as a human being and the society has her as a women. Our society is full of absurdity and contradictions and here a female is considered as a marginal member of the family, both in her parent house as well as in husbands.

Throughout her life span, she is unable to fix on her roots and this leads to her insecurity. Therefore, through her writings she brings out the inner life of women and protest against gender supremacy. Among Indian woman writers, Deshpande is specifically committed to the restructuring of female subjectivity.

Deshpande's concerns related to the feminist questions are important in the interest of an Indian feminist-praxis. Her fictions holds a great promise and helps us in finding ways in which the historical 'location' of Indian women can be interpreted in terms of their subordination accentuated by law, sacred literature and practice. Deshpande's feminist ideology approaches towards women's empowerment. She refuses to indulge in adversarial orientation or intemperate expressions towards men.

Deshpande's treatment of issues like Indian woman's autonomy, identity, space and desire may lead to an Indian model of feminism which will be workable, honest and more violable for indigenous condition. The contemporary women are facing structural inequalities between men and women and cultural rationalization of these inequalities. Anil Kumar Gupta in his book *Woman and Society* mentions that the discrimination based on gender differences are interlocked and every level of society from the most intimate to the most general.

Deshpande deals with women's conditioning in relation to their choice of career. They seem to be bound within the traditional roles of caring, curing and nurturing. Through their natural capacities of compassion and nurturance the society circumscribes them to specific roles whereas there are plenty of avenues for men in where one can see diversity and change.

A picture is worth a thousand words. But each novel by Deshpande is worth a thousand pictures. That is what makes her a celebrated writer, says Hanifa Ghosh: "Celebrations", an essay published and printed in the pages of the Indian review of books a couple of years ago, highlighted the essence of Deshpande's writing – incisive, rational but spontaneous. The early years of her marriage were largely given over to the care of her two young sons but she took a course in journalism and for a time worked on a magazine.

Deshpande has created an authentic female characters flesh and blood characters with recognizable credentials. She depicts the Indian women's life in all her novels. Her writings are characterized by a racy style, Sari says in *The Dark Hold No Terrors* : 'Silence had been a habit for us'. Indu in *Roots and Shadows* says about her cold relationship with Jeyant that 'I am passive and unresponsive. I'm still and dead'. Likewise in all her works silence is the key metaphor.

Many of her themes are similar to those of recent European and American Women's fiction, particularly in the description of various stages of a women's life. Her fiction reveals some influence of the Bronte sisters, Jane Austen, Margaret Drabble, and Doris Lessing and Erica Jong. Generally, Deshpande is engaged in creating, new self-hood for her characters in all her novels. She draws sustenance from tradition and trying to arrive at a resolution for the dilemma for her characters whether to seek identity apart from traditional role within the family structure. She has woven a delicate and subtle texture into her fictional world with a good deal of thought and dexterity.

The chief concern in Deshpande's novel is the self-assessment of the protagonist themselves. She is compelling urge for a way of loving which will respond to the inner most earnings of women for freedom and self dignity. She employs her writings as a vehicle to probe into women's lives and experiences. She has portrayed the inner turmoil of a woman fighting within herself between her own knowledge and the philosophy thrust on her by the surroundings.

Her women display a determination to face the riddles of life boldly. The continuous analysis of their own self enables them to understand and solve their problems. Her novels will give the readers a clear idea about the social milieu, the problems of women, and the solutions they find for the problems.

Deshpande does not encourage her female protagonists to rise in rebellion against the males in family matters. Instead, she wants to build a harmonious relationship between man and woman in a spirit of give and take, in a mood of compromise and reconciliation.

A proper co-ordination, a reasonable mutual understanding between husband and wife is essential for a happy married life. This is the clear-cut marriage of Deshpande.

Deshpande's novels are written by specialists eminent in their own fields. The collection of essays offers new insights into the novels of Deshpande and the scholarly exercise of the authors provide new and meaningful approach to her novels and the issues generated by the novelist together give the readers an opportunity to understand the novelist's predominant themes in a better perspective. As a living writer in India, Deshpande reflects a realistic picture of the contemporary middle class family life. Her writings transcend gender boundaries. Human issues are relevant in her writings. Humanity is her concern.

Deshpande's novels deal with the women belonging to Indian middle class, who are brought up in a traditional environment and are struggling to liberate themselves and seek their self-identity and independence. She is also the one and only contemporary writer who have given graphic details about the girl-child and her psychology. Simone De Beauvoir writes : "One is not born but rather becomes, a woman...," it is civilization as a whole that produces this creature..., described as feminine. (Shashi Deshpande's Novels : (1).

Deshpande gives minute details of the development of girl-child in her novels. In *Roots and Shadows* she has displayed a series of girl-children, where each girl faces a different problem within the family circle. Deshpande has given us the glimpse of the rigid system of marriage in India which is decided not on the basis compatibility but on caste, religion and dowry. Basically she writes about the condition of women and their failures and depression in the fast changing socio-economic milieu of India. She writes about the clash between tradition and modernity in relation to women in the middle class society. Her depiction of women's world is realistic, authentic and credible which showcases the gender supremacy and gender politics in our patriarchal society.

Deshpande does believe that she is a feminist and her concerns are universal. She writes about silent, sobbing women-mothers, grandmothers, aunts, sisters, grand-aunts, daughters and a whole lot of females. Probably the author herself is aware of, too many thronging the pages of the novel.

The main theme in her novels is not the facile one of opposing tradition with modernity or westernization with Indian culture. Her character grapple with their struggle which drags them through innocence and experience, ignorance and knowledge girlhood and adulthood, repression and submission and rebellion, joy and sorrow that lends her novels an elemental sweep, simple as the surface text be. Deshpande life as a girl is an integral part of an adult life. She recognizes the childhood influences and tendencies and in time of crisis her characters turn back to the past to search for reasons within and in the family.

Deshpande's fiction is an example of the ways in which a girl child's particular position, social reality and psychological growth determine her personality. She argues that it would be psychological unrealistic to imagine that awareness within them women emerges suddenly, that she becomes a 'person' with the onset adolescence. The role of early life experiences, the role of education, closeness to parents, sibling relationships are some very crucial elements that go a long way in creating a woman's personality.

With a gift for sharp psychological insight into the subtleties of human mind and society and aided by a richly evocative, unassuming and unpretentious style, Shashi Deshpande is ideally suited to tread the labyrinthine traits of human psyche and creditably represent it in fiction.

Deshpande, an eminent novelist has emerged as a writer possessing deep insight into the female psyche. Focusing on the marital relations, she seeks to expose the tradition by which a woman is trained to play her subservient role in the family. Her novels reveal the man-made patriarchal traditions and the uneasiness of the modern Indian woman in being a part of them.

Deshpande is not only articulated a thematic and technical maturity but also effectively communicates an intensely apprehended feminine sensibility. She has apparently injected a new consciousness, offering varied interpretation of imperishable Indian values as well as highlighting our cultural heritage. She added a new depth and a new dimension to Indian English Fiction. She repeatedly calls for understanding and balance in matrimony, however not at the cost of one's self-respect and individuality. Her novels based on submission and sufferings of women do not necessarily end with their rejection of family values and marriage. Her bold and balanced heroines are often facing the challenges of life confidently.

Mostly they return to their husbands with the realization that self-assertion and conformity to one's given role are not contradictory, but can even be complementary. Thus, the end shows them as women aware f the importance of family and marriage, at the same time, accepting their need to discover their 'self'.

Deshpande is the author of four children's books and seven novels. Her novels are *The Dark Holds No Terror (1980), If I Die Today (1982), The Binding Vine (1982), Come up and Be Dead (1983), Roots and Shadows (1983), That Long Silence (1988) and A Matter of Time (1996)*.

Deshpande's short stories were published in magazine such as Femina, Eve's Weekly etc. The legacy, the first of her short stories came out in 1978 and in 1980. Her first novel, *The Dark Holds No Terrors* was published in June 1980. The feminist press of New York brought out her latest novel *A Matter of Time* her first work to be published in the USA. *The Dark Holds No Terrors and Roots and Shadows* have received major awards like Nanjangud Thirumalamba Award and Thirumathi Rangammal prize in 1991 and 1984. It was translated into German and Russian. This novel built around the metaphor of the dark and the light. It is about male ego wherein the male refuses to play a second fiddle role in marriage.

Small Remedies is a complex novel. It is a novel about myriad feelings love, courage, honesty, truth, trust, death and pain. It is also the novels, which clearly marks the development of the personal philosophy of the writer. Here she envisages a hopeful future for women in their "shared experiences as women". It is a woman's journey towards self-realization. This theme of woman's quest for self forms the crux of almost all her works. It tells the story of Madhu Sptarishi, whose search for identity of two other women – Savitri Bai Indorekar and Leela. It is through their struggle for identity that Madhy comes to know her own self. It projects the quest for self-recitation of Indian women in a hostile patriarchal society. It is the novel of past and present intermingled.

Roots and Shadows started out to be a detective novel. It depicts the agony and suffocation experienced by the protagonist in a male-dominated and tradition-bound society. In this she displayed a girl who faces a different problem within the family circle. Because of gender politics, the heroine Indu utters her hobby of writing but alters her life-style to please her husband and the main reason behind this is writing is considered as a male-coded profession. She eventually becomes a submissive wife to a domineering husband. It also presents another facet of deprived womanhood through the character Akka, who is the youngest sister of Indu's grandfather. Mini inculcated in her all the traditional feminine qualities since her childhood.

The BindingWine, her fourth novel deals with the personal tragedy of the protagonist, condition of women in this novel is very miserable. In this novel, Urmila stands apart from the rest of Deshpande's Female protagonists because she is a liberated woman. It depicts the pain and repress experienced by the protagonist. It uses the personal tragedy of the narrator Urmi to focus attention on victims like Kalpana and Mira-Victims of man's lust and woman's helplessness.

If I Die Today and *Come Up and Be Dead* contain a lot of thrill and suspense in them, and they clearly betray Deshpande's readings in Agatha Christie and Sherlock Homes. The narrator Manju is quite different from the average Indian woman who views matrimony and motherhood as the ultimate happiness in life. It also lays bare the feeble male ego, which cannot tolerate the idea of female superiority. The predicaments of men and women are hailing from a middle class milieu. In *Come up and Be Dead,* women characters are typically the modern idea of freedom and the traditional need for a husband and home of their own.

Stone Woman is a sincere attempt at discovering complexities in the minds of women. *Death of a Child* deals with the problem of a woman's unwanted pregnancy and her subsequent decision to get it terminated. While probing into the minds of her characters she probes into her own self as she says, "In discovering other women, I have discovered myself".

In *A Matter of Time*, Shashi Deshpande for the first time enters into the metaphysical world of philosophy. It is an exploration of a women inner life. It explored different dimensions of women's experience in India. She believes her work is having an impact on women's lives. Here the inner life of women emotionally isolated from her family is reflected and refracted in the embryonic women represented by her daughters. Human relationship is the main theme of this outstanding novel.

Deshpande tries to exonerate the male by bringing in some strong, loving and responsible figures. This particularly deals with the main theme of the quest for a female identity. Her fourth novel for children, *The Narayanpur Incident*, is based on quit India movement and the role of children in it. These novels are readable and the last of them made a great impact on the world of children's literature. In respect of technique also these stories contain the germs of most of the strengths and limitations of her novels.

Deshpande's novels present at times a lonely and somber world. They reflect, according to Muriel was, "unhappy realities of Indian life" and the woman's "depressing, Melancholic or catastrophic world..." It is time for Deshpande, "she concludes to open some of her windows and let the morning light till her dark rooms". Women's struggle is clearly visualized in the context of contemporary Indian society, to find and preserve her identity as wife, mother and most important of all. Deshpande's chief concern as a creative writer and this appears in all her important stories. (Calcutta : Writer worksop 10). The blind dominance of man upon woman has motivated a discussion of the slavish life of women.

In *That Long Silence*, Jaya, the central character does not have the liberty to express her suffering even in her writings. In fact there has been a great need for interest in works and the subject in Deshpande, Shobha De have dealt with issues related to women.

That Long Silence, acclaimed masterpiece of feminist writing in Indo-English fiction raises the status of Deshpande, among the writers of the present day. This highlights the image of middle class women sandwiches between tradition and modernity. This is her most autobiographical novel. It won the Sahitya Academy Award in 1990. It tells the story of an Indian housewife, who maintains silence throughout her life. The novel ends with her resolve to speak, who maintains silence throughout her life. The novel ends with her resolve to speak, to break her long silence. The metaphor of silence under which the novel is organized helps t impose the inner dynamics of a self-cut off from a human communication.

Indian women are struggling to adjust with it rather than get free from the conventional world. Women have always been fighting for equal recognition in society. When the reader across her fiction her feelings and perceptions with an astuteness and a creativity that came across like a breath of fresh air. Deshpande's persevering search for 'self' in her novels shows that she has largely confined herself to the problems of patriarchy which fully occupied with the gender politics and it revolves around gender supremacy.

S.P.Swain observes:

The tragic predicament of the Deshpande protagonists is the outcome of male-domination in a patriarchal culture. Their silent suffering is socio-psychic in nature. In her quest for identity, the Deshpande protagonist moves from despair to hope, from self-negation to self-assertion. Her struggle throughout is to attain wholeness, completeness and an authentic selfhood." (125).

Deshpande tries to divulge the delicate process of intimidation and gender discrimination at work in the family and in the male oriented society. One of the aspects of their upbringing is their inculcation as girls into the socially defined roles as daughter, wife and mother. Deshpande shows immense sympathy and consciousness of the ways and means through which a young girl is prepared for her future status in society. The features that influence her include cultural aspects and social and psychological factors. Her major acknowledged novels *That Long Silence* and *Roots and Shadows* deal with the search for Gender Specific self-definition of women, who are educated and modern but cannot quite discard their surrounding and the mode in which they have been brought up continuously. Gender roles are visualized, examined and enacted within an amalgam of relationships. Monika states that:

Feminism can be classified as a political perception based on two fundamental premises, one is based on gender differences is the foundation of the structural inequality between men and women by which women suffer systematic social injustice and the second focuses the inequality between the sexes is not the result of biological necessity but is produced by the cultural construction of gender differences. This provides feminism with its double program: to understand the social and psychic mechanism that constructs and perpetuates gender inequality and then to change them …. Feminism is a consciously held ideology, which opposes consciously held ideologies that maintain the primacy of masculine authority and power. (Monica 76)

TWO

FEMININE MYSTIQUE IN THAT LONG SILENCE

The importance of women has been recognized in literature on various grounds. For centuries, the human experience has been synonymous with the masculine experience. Gyno- criticism has opened up new vistas of study and research. The feminist philosophy projects the problem of "self" The quest of women's identity is a typical motif of feminist literature and a central task of feminist literacy criticism.

Accordingly Deshpande's novels reflecting their high erect mind of women's identity seem to reveal the essential and typical theme of feminist literature. Deshpande's novels show how the "feminine mystique" deceives women, and that the persona a wise mother and good wife, is no more women's desirable identity And it is presented through a heroine who suffers from the inner dissociation and attempts to wander outside the house.

In some respects, Simone de Beauvoir's sharp observation affirms that "He is the Subject, he is the absolute and she is the "Other" sums up why the self is an important issue in feminism. To be the "Other" is to be the non-person, the non-subject, the non-agent-in short, the mere representation of body. Deeming women are emotional and unprincipled, these thinkers advocated confining women to the domestic sphere where their wives could be neutralized, even transformed into virtues, in the role of submissive wife and nurturing mother.

A major preoccupation in recent Indian women's writing has been a delineation of inner life and subtle interpersonal relationships. In an ethnicity where individualism have often protest remained alien ideas, and marital bliss and the women's role at home is a central focus; it is interesting to see the coming out ideas which is not just an essential Indian sensibility but an expression of cultural displacement.

Deshpande has joined the growing number of women writers from boundaries has significant impact. The finite dimension of the relationship between man and woman has been prescribed by man and not by women. Man who is ruled by the mastery –motive has imposed her limits on her. She accepts it because of bio-social reasons. Very often, this acceptance is not congruent with the reality that lies underneath. Modern women prefer to exercise-her choice and break away from her traumatic experiences.

Women are now portrayed as more assertive, more liberated in their view, and more articulate in their expression then the women of the past .Instead of downgrading the elements of suffering at the hands of her lover or husband or man, she has started asserting her substantive identity in action, not in words. Whether it is Devi of Githa Hariharan's *The Thousand Faces of Night or Sita of Shashi Desphande The Dark Holds No Terrors or Lucy of J.M.Coetzee's Disgrace,* the women have established coherent class structure-one of assertion of identity and defiance of male supremacy, and protest at protest at being subordinated by man.

The male ego has given the women an inferior status through the ages. Man has relegated her to a second-class citizen. A group of Indian women novelist's in their, hybridism of thought and multi-cultural, multi-lingual and multi-religious social dimensions have conceptualized the women problem in general and middle-class and upper-class women in particular.

While the gynocritics think that too many women in too many countries speak the same language of silence, some Indian women novelists like Geetha Hariharan, Shashi Deshpande, Arunthathi Roy, and Anitha Desi have tried with sincerity and honesty to deal with the physical, psychological and emotional stress syndrome of women.

Deshpande began her literary career in 1977 as a short story writer. She is a born story teller who proved her sustained creativity the novel form. She is one of the widely read post-independence Indian English writers who write consciously of the issues that concerned that educated middle class women in Indian society. She attempts to closely analyze man-women relationship within the perimeters of family and the contemporary social set-up. She primarily focuses on the captivating problems and the suffocating environs of her heroine's, who struggle hard in this malicious and callous male-dominated world to discover the true identity.

Deshpande has thrashed women's problems and situations in a fast-changing social scenario. We cannot brand her either has typical western liberated or an orthodox Indian one. She does not let herself be overwhelmed by the western feminism or its militant concept of liberation. In quest for wholeness of identity, she does not advocate separation from the diplomatic assertion of one's identity within marriage.

In spite of the advances in technology and science, society still marginalizes women, based on gender distinction .In our society, there is a distorted notion that if somebody writes anything about women would be a feminist writers worked out on the exaggerated or fabricated troubles of women and at the end of the story the protagonist quarrels with the male characters and publicly challenges the male domination.

Deshpande differs from other feminist writers on the angle. She does not write as a feminist but she has a women's perceptive on her works. She deals with the genuine problems of contemporary Indian women. With her works she could convey the depths of female psyche. Her protagonists are modern, educated young women, crushed under the weight of a male dominated and tradition bound society. Her attempts to give an honest portrayal of their sufferings, disappointments and frustrations makes her novels 'feminist texts'.

Deshpande does not make her women characters stronger than they actually are in their real life. We can see the elements of Deshpande heroines in every women of today's Indian society. They hold the authenticity of flesh and blood. Deshpande has specially selected these characters from real life and readers can equate these characters with themselves or somebody they know.

By describing women characters with a feminist awareness, she reveals her own attitude the concepts of liberation. Her writings therefore lend themselves to a feminist interpretation, which is not necessarily based on western type feminisms. Her female protagonist redefined the sati-savithri image. She tries to re-evaluate the present Indian values system and recommends the importance of equality in man-women relationship.

On this aspect, she has portrayed the 'bossy' nature of men and pointed out that women are turned to be mere secretaries after their marriage. A typical Indian husband considers his wife as a machine, which speed up or smoothen his day to day work. For the marriage is the means for them marriage is a means for their social and personal betterment. After accepting dowry they use their wives as unpaid servants; Indian husbands gain more from the 'marriage sale'.

Deshpande generally has the heroine as the narrator, and employs a kind of stream of consciousness technique. All the novels of Deshpande hold the power to deliver the problems of middle class women in a genuine sense. Her novels conceive the elements of personal experiences. Her psychological insight into her characters put her on par with the masters of the genre.

Deshpande have a peculiar authenticity, as they seem to be direct offshoots of their peculiar backgrounds. They don't speak much but we have ample opportunity to read their minds of even their inner feelings. Deshpande has a rare vitality of language to make her portraits striking as well as convincing. Deshpande writes in a clear, lucid prose. Her articulation of thoughts is done in such a way that the reader feels a bond with her. We feel as if she has stolen our feelings and thoughts and return about them. Her finely honed sensibility reflects the wonderful interplay of relationships and also many facts of isolation. The ambience is the everyday world with its hustle and bustle.

The novelists do not indulge in verbal acrobatics, she does not believe in beating round the bush. Technique is very important for her. She directly hits the nail on the head in her fiction. This clarity of perception is visible when she categorically gives definitions of love and marriage. Right from the beginning of their life; women are forced to feel dwarfed and acquire a highly circumscribed world-view. Bolinger utters, "Women taught their place along with other lesser breeds by the implicit life that language tells about them" (15). This unfortunate state of affairs has been responsible for many problems and confusions which women have been condemned to face.

It may be mentioned at the outset that while dealing with her female character, especially their relations with men, their drives and responses and their sexual repression, Deshpande has made significant efforts to step out of the main current narrative devices and linguistic technique as developed by the masculine approach. She has tried to look at things essentially from the women's point of view.

Although writing for her, is not an act of deliberation, reason and choice and is primarily a matter of instinct, Deshpande is fully aware of the possibilities of her medium and seems to be making at times strenuous efforts to explore its possibilities. Her earnest attempts to break new grounds have made their linguistically self conscious, she keeps on trying to annex. Like a resource full poet new verbal domains had integrate varying notes of perception and writing. Whether she succeeds or not in her efforts, one thing that is certain is that she is almost invariably eager to exploit various linguistic resources at her disposal.

Social conformity has always been obligatory for a woman than for a man. Generally, a woman's identity tends to be defined by others. Due to her sensitive nature, Jaya is very particular about molding her tastes in order to suit those of the rest even if her superior intellect is not satisfied. In the very beginning of the novel, we see that she tries to reason out with her father as to why pressing her desire. Here, Deshpande has presented the theme of lack of communication, as she herself declares that the themes of lack of communication may be over-familiar in western fiction, but in extrovert India it is not much analyzed.

In the novels under study, Deshpande presents the meanings of silence. As she mentions: "You learn a lot of tricks to get by in a relationship. Silence is one of them. You never find a woman criticizing her husband, even playfully, in case it might damage the relationship(Sandhu sarbjit,1991,40) Deshpande brings out the universal problem of women in the world through the characters of Jaya, the protagonist in *That Long Silence.*

Jaya, the central character plays a significant role in depicting the inner suffering and feelings of women in an Indian society. Though exposed to modernity, certain Indian women feel that they are somehow subordinate to the male members of the society. Jaya is one such character who longs for complete freedom but fails to attain it because gender supremacy, still hopes to get it.

Suman Ahuja reviewing the novel for The Times of India observes that "Jaya caught in an emotional eddy, endeavors to come to terms with her protean roles, while trying albeit in vain, to rediscover her true self, which is but a ephemera of unfulfilled wife, a disappointed mother and a failed writer (2).

The heroine of the *That Long Silence,* Jaya, can be called a mouth piece of Shashi Deshpande herself. The way of thinking and opinions of Jaya is indisputably that of Deshpande. Her fifth novel, *That Long Silence* teaches the reader that the real empowerment comes from our inner will and the capacity to reach beyond restricted and guarded forts. She successfully makes her readers realize that all path-breaking discoveries are the outcome of faith, which helps, mankind like a ladder to reach the zenith. The journey to wider horizons requires an innovative effort. What she has said in *That Long Silence is* true of all times in the history of mankind:

To achieve something, to become anything, you've got to be hard and truth less. Yes, even if you want to be a saint, if you want to love the whole world, you've got to stop loving individual human beings first. And if they love you, and they bleed when you show them you don't love them not specially, well, so much the worse for them! There's just no other way of being a saint. Or a painter, A writer, (1).

Male characters do not have any prominent role in Deshpande's novels. The reader can easily find out resemblance in Deshpande's heroes and sometimes they even look monotonous. She presents these characters only as dominating male characters seems to produce them only to trouble the women in her fiction. As Sara Grimke puts it: Man has subjugated women to his will used her as a means of selfish gratification, to minister to his sexual pleasure, to be instrumental in promoting his comfort; but never he desired to elevate her to that she was created to fill.

Jaya's decision to exercise her rights is a welcome one. She wants to liberate herself by respecting her feelings and desires. Kamini Dinesh finds " Jaya moving out of the 'cloistered self' as she seeks to escape from the struggles of everyday life and is forced to find inner resources that will allow her to return and engage more fully in her life and marriage". (196) Jaya's optimistic view of life that changes are possible, exposes the transformation she has undergone.

Jaya's husband, Mohan was that sort of a man and he married her for his social betterment. Jaya had lost her father at the age of fifteen and her brother considered her a burden and this lead her to marry Mohan. Before her marriage, Jaya had been thought the importance of the husband in the life of women. Vanithamani tells her that a husband is a sheltering tree.

Ramukaka reminds her of the think that the happiness of her husband and home depends entirely on her. When Jaya is leaving her home after her marriage, Dada has advised her to "be good to

Mohan". Jaya's brother brought Mohan with money and gave him to Jaya and she tried to be good to him. This was the beginning of Jaya's lifeless kind of married life.

The silence of woman symbolizes helplessness. But men take it as a symbol of woman's contentment. Rashmi Gaur observes:

"Jaya's journey towards a well-defined self-hood is mired in the labyrinthine mazes of societal pressures, feminine conditioning to fashion oneself according to the accepted norms of behavior, suppressive and egotistic male chauvinism and the continued dilemma of attaching a purpose to her life, culmination in a long silence. Her silence is symptomatic of alienation and apprehension rioted in every woman's soul in different forms - a silence which is often misunderstood by men as a symbol of woman's contentment". (179).

The entire novel brings out the stale married life in a middle class home and Deshpande tells the story from the point of view of a wife. The women in Mohan's family were so definite about their roles and duties. But Jaya has no clear cut idea about her role in that family. Her life before marriage and after marriage shared little similarity. Her father gave her the name 'Jaya' for 'victory'. But her in-laws gave her a new name 'Suhasini' pointed to a docile but efficient housewife.

Concerned only about the tastes and interests of Mohan, Jaya has lost her authenticity as a human being. She has changed herself to the wishes of Mohan. Mohan kept her away from her likings. She was forced by Mohan to given up the job she wanted to take, the baby she wanted to adopt and the anti-price campaign she had wanted to take part in. Jaya's journey through the rough road of her nuptial life, She at last: "no questions, no retorts: only silence". In accepting everything mutely, she thinks she resembles Sita or Draupadi. In her view, The truth is that it was Mohan, who had a clear idea of What he wanted; the kind of life he wanted to lead, the kind of home he would live in, and I went along with him (25).

Deshpande's Women-centered novels and short stories give us a psychological insight into the working of a women's mind. Ever since Jaya got married, she has done nothing but wait.

The novel depicts the life of Jaya at the level of the silent and the unconscious.

A sensitive and realistic dramatization of the married life of Jaya and her husband Mohan, it portrays an inquisitive critical appraisal to which the institution of marriage has been subjected to in recent years.

Since her childhood, Jaya has been designed her life according to the desires of the members of her family. Her father is very fascinated with Paluskar and Faiyazkhan, but she is very fascinated with Lata Mangeshkar, but the film music is banned in her house, so her father remarks on her "what poor taste you have, Jaya" (TLS:3) made her feel ashamed of herself. She has neither courage nor will to justify her own choice, and this is the beginning of her predicament.

No wonder Jaya learns to suppress her own wishes and act according to her husband's wish. Jaya loves compassionate life depicted in advertisement, which proceed in the movie show. She thinks that her husband's too comment her for having such a taste. Jaya feels herself to be trodden worm as she has been restrained for years of submission to Mohan. She wants to share equal responsibility and liberty as "a pair of bullocks yoked together" (TLS : 7) but her life is meant to perform household duties. She feels that it is a clear phrase but cannot be substituted for the reality because a woman has to go behind her husband.

In Indian society the authority to decide, to plan, to organize life is an act done by men. Mohan is also a typical Indian husband who wants to decide everything on his own.

"The truth is that it was Mohan, who had a clear idea of what he wanted to lead, the kind of home he would live in, and I went along with him (TLS : 25).

No doubt Mohan encourages her to write but the way he expects. Her writing is also a kind of breaking the silence. Rajeswarisunder Rajan argues, Deshpande's protagonist breaks her silence at one level through the act of writing itself, at another level through renegotiation interpersonal relations within the family" (876-88).

Jaya says that their life is being led by Mohan, her husband, and she has to follow him without revealing her likes and dislikes. Mohan himself does not give the chance for her to decide. Even the sound of women give a disturbing feeling to men, this is substantiated when Nayana talks feebly to Jaya when Mohan is around "As if even the sound of our voices would be an affront to the male" (TLS : 27). There is no right to woman to woman to talk as she wishes.

A girl child is subjugated to all sorts of tortures and torments in the society. So Nayana's craving for a male child is not for her love towards male members of the society. But she feels that, "Why give birth to a girl, bennji, who'll only suffer because of men all her life? Look at me! My mother loved me very much, she wanted so much for me........ a house with electricity and water, shining brass vessels, a silver waist chain, silver anklets...... And what I got? No, no, behniji, better to have a son (TLS : 28).

Nayana wants even her unborn child to be boy because there will be no suffering to it like her, instead he will dominate others; she herself is unaware of the possibility that a female has the capability to dominate the male, because she has been accustomed to such a male dominated society.

Jaya says that every woman has to tolerate and subjugate herself. She has been doing nothing but waiting for one thing or other. She herself tells that: "Yes, Even since I got married, I had done nothing but wait. Waiting for Mohan to come home, waiting for the children to be born, for them to start school, waiting for them to come" home, waiting for the milk, the servant, the lunch-carrier man....., and above and beyond this, there had been for me that other waiting ..., waiting fearfully for disaster, for a catastrophe. (TLS : 30). Fourteen years of Jaya's married life is spending doing nothing, but waiting.

Right from the beginning there is a blind belief that a husband is the one who has the capability to protect and safeguard the family with his proper planning. Therefore he is called as sheltering tree.

They fail to think that a woman has the same capability. She is all the time made dependent and follow him like a shadow. Vanitamani advises Jaya that she has to obey her husband because he is like a sheltering tree, but Jaya ignores the ideas of Vanitamani.

The crucial point here is that Vanitamani even though she is a woman wants Jaya to be dependent to her husbands, because Vanitamani has been leading a life of suppression for many years. Mohan blames Jaya and his children for the corruption committed by him. He says that it is for her sake and his children's sake he had done all those wrong things.

A woman stepping into the marital life is like stepping into the life of subordination, suppression. She is completely dominated by her husband. The clash between husband and wife arises because of irregular sharing of ideas. Jaya faces the same problem. She never enjoys her identity. In every action she has to follow her husband. "I'm Mohan's wife I had thought, and cut off the bits of me that had refused to be Mohan's wife (TLS : 191).

Even she turns herself as the blind eye towards her husband's illegal earning and corrupt practices. Sita following her husband into exile Savitri dogging death to reclaim her husband, Draupadi stoically sharing her husband's travils..., No, what have I to do with these mythical women? I can't fool myself. The truth is simpler. Two bullocks yoked together..., it is more comfortable for them to move in the same direction. To go in different directions would be painful; and what animal would voluntarily choose pain? (TLS : 11).

Jaya does not want to follow her husband in blind folded way. She has all sorts of revolutionary ideas to oppose her husband but she fails to put it in actions. She is not ready to be a typical Indian wife like Sita and Draupadi. She wants her life to be like "two bullocks yoked together" with Mohan. She thinks that the relationship between husband and wife should be mutual and they should share equal rights. There should not be inferiority or superiority among them. This is so because there is no love and mutual understanding between them.

Jaya seems to have almost nothing to ask in her life. Deshpande concretizes Jaya's plight in the well-known childhood bed-time story of the wise sparrow who built a house of wax and the foolish crow who built hers of dung on a rainy night the crow's house collapses forcing her to seek shelter at the sparrows. The sparrow is so possessive of and attached to her home that she keeps to crow waiting, out in the rain, for a considerable time. She allows the crow in only when she is thoroughly drenched and then guides her to the hot pan to warm her. The foolish crow hopes onto it and gets burnt to death.

Jaya and variety of other female figures, in generations of women in her family (Jaya, her mother, her grandmother); among different classes of women in same generation (Jaya her cousin Kusum, her widowed neighbor Mukta), have all been trained in silence. The whole novel depicts the life of Jaya at the level of the silent and the unconscious. It is the story of women who undergoes some mental torture and suffering at the hands of her husband.

The protagonist Jaya gets an outlet of her suppressed feeling by writing. Mohan takes pride in her writings but strongly oppose it her themes which he feels to have her autobiographical overtones. He never encourages her, neither loves it, instead of that he tells, "They will all know now, all those people who read this and know this and know us, they will know that these persons are us, they will think I am this kind of man, they will know I am this man. How can I look anyone in the face again? And you how could you write these think (TLS : 143).

Mohan does not want to spoil his image. He says that writings of Jaya will spoil it and he feels awkward to face the society because the society will have a bad impression on him after reading Jaya, because she has dealt about her suppressed life. He questions her how she can write such matters publicly. This act of Mohan shows that he dominates Jaya to the core. She does not have liberty even in a fictitious world.

Jaya realizes the selfish nature of Mohan. She worries for it but she does not oppose Mohan, instead she keeps silent because from her childhood she has learnt that a husband is like a sheltering tree, a protector and security for a woman, therefore these speeches make her remain silent.

Jaya is dissatisfied with her married life because she is often lost in contemplation about her childhood, girlhood and womanhood. Moreover, the fault is not on her side first she has to take the reconciliatory step after days of Mohan's stubborn silence. Soon after that Jaya instead of raising her voice in protest becomes a silent segregated woman, because she has learnt to live under the shell of silence. Often she feels wounded and hurt at the pile of accusation on her, she is struck dumb, and she wonders, "Oh god, why could not I speak? Why couldn't I say something! I couled say nothing?" (TLS : 119).

Mohan wants to marry "a girl who can speak English". Mohan has married Jaya not out of love but she resembled his dream girl when she talked fluently in English. Jaya adds reason for her silence and submissive nature. She says, Mohan wanted a well-educated woman not a reciprocating and loving women. He, himself acknowledged that, "You know Jaya, the first day I met you at your Ramakaku's house, you were talking to your brother, Dinkar and Somehow you sounded so much like that girl, I think it was at the moment that I decided I would marry you". (TLS : 90).

He expected a girl who can speak English and he married Jaya, not out of love but because she resembles the dream girl when she talked fluently in English. Therefore after their marriage there is no mutual love but only the disheartening life, so both of them are living together but there had been only emptiness between them. So out of social fear Jaya and Mohan continue to bed husband and wife. Marriage subjugates and enslaves woman and it leaves them into mental suffering and it leads her into very sorrowful stage, but she tolerate everything. Mohan does not share any devotional love towards her, though she does not want to reject her role as wife and mother, without these two there is no life for her.

In this novel women are shown as bundles of suffering. Not only Jaya undergoes such subordination but also Mohan's mother, who has been victimized by his father's temperamental explosion in which the food served to him; the lacking in fresh chutney is thrown on the wall and mother has to prepare it again in the late night. Mohan, while narrating this incident to Jaya, appreciates his mother's endurance and silence also calls it as a quality of an ideal wife. But Jaya feels that the woman maintains silence bitterly. It is unendurable and also formidable silence.

He saw strength in the woman sitting silently in front of the fire, but I saw despair. I saw despair so great that it would not voices itself. I saw a struggle so bitter that silence was the only weapon silence and surrender. I'am woman and I can understand her better; he's a man and he can't (TLS : 37).

Mohan sees strength and endurance in his mother whereas Jaya sees despair and grief followed by bitter silence. She also says that a man cannot understand the depressed emotions of woman where as it is easy for a woman to experience the sorrow of another woman. Sarabjit sandhu remarks: "Mohan is a traditionalist rooted in customs. To him, a women sitting in front of the fire, waiting for her husband to come and eat hot food is the real ' strength' of a women". (40)

Mohan expects a strong traditional background where he had grown up seeing his mother silently submit to every erotic demand of his father with the roles of submissive wife and dominating husband deeply ingrained in his mind, he enters into matrimony with Jaya. Jaya is the only daughter of an unconventional family, adored by her father and brothers. This leads to the clash between Jaya and Mohan. Mohan followed the footsteps of his father, who was a tyrant, and drunken, who could not understand the feeling and desires of his wife.

"My mother never raised her voice against my father, however badly he behaved to her". (83) His mother had silently endured the moods of her drunkard husband and slogged to fulfill his irrational demands. Jaya and Mohan both are brought in different angle, but Jaya tries to adjust with her husband but Mohan wants to dominate his wife.

In her seventeen years of married life, Jaya never lived a single moment for her. She is all the time referred as someone's wife and someone's mother. She sacrificed her entire life for her family. At this juncture she feels that her individuality is refused.

According to Jaya that female infanticide is better, than to live in this male dominated world. She recollects the violent act done to kill the female infants,

Where was it I had read an account of how baby girls were done to death a century or so back? They were, I had read in horror, buried alive, cursed to death in the room they were born in; and immediately after that, a fire was lit on the spot to purify the place, they said. Perhaps it was to endure death. And those agonies.., for days I had been unable to get it out of my mind. But now I wondered where it wasn't more merciful, that swift ending of the agony once and for all, than this prolonging of it for years and years. (53)

Jaya after undergoing a long life of suffering and suppression, thinks that it is better to perish the female in its infant's stage because as an adult she has to endure everything and adjust with everyone, even she has to sacrifice all things for her family but the society never considers her as one of the soul in the world. She says that it is acceptable to die than to lead a life of prolonging agony.

Jaya picks up the threads of her past and tries to connect it with her present, she recollects the triumph with her present, with which her father had named her Jaya,

"Jaya for victory" (15). Her father's death ironically, symbolizes the beginnings of her defeat. This conflict between her dual indentifies leaves her confused and uncertain. When her husband renames Jaya she simply maintains silence because she doesn't want to arise any questions against her husband. Mohan never tries to know Jaya's expectations and desires. This makes Jaya to keep her association with Kamat she finds with the good companion which she misses in Mohan. Even his behaviour makes Jaya a good ideal friend. She also gets some solace from Kamat which she fails to get from her husband. Kamat treats him as best friend and great well wisher even he encourages her reminiscent of an elder brother.

A kind of friendship between married woman and another man is always looked upon with suspicion and disapproval. Jaya is a role model of Indian married women's mind. Her friend Kamat encourages Jaya to write and chides her for avoidance of life in her writing for this she feels a love that is more than gratitude, love which falls outside the conventional boundaries.

Though she has heartfelt feelings, she neglects to speak out and runs away from the place the moment she sees Kamat's dead body. This incident underlines how marriage often derives people into impossible and embarrassed situations. Jaya cannot even stay and pay homage to her best friend in his death for the gender politics. Perhaps she does her role of wife in a perfect manner, but fails as a human being. The wisdom that Jaya derives in this situation is to follow her will and act accordingly. If we focus our attention on the propriety or justifiability of her will or ego, the result may be mixed. Her conduct is not the model of righteousness or even right, she may be wrong or very wrong, but she is human and her reaction has a feminine modern quality, making her modern or new women without abjuring the totality of the obligations of the typically traditional women in India.

As the title of the novel indicates, Jaya for very long in her past life tried to play the role of traditional women, the embodiment of tolerance ,suffering and courage .However, her courage deserts her and she becomes the modern egotistical self – assertive rebellious women – all this being marks of modern feminist awakening. However, the desertion of the traditional submissive role and adoption of the new role do not leave the psyche of Jaya unstinted and intact. She is in great emotional turmoil. It is this emotional turmoil and suffering that the novelist depicts with rare skill.

When the human ego sinks into the flood of sufferings and its power of toleration reaches the brink of negation, freedom to act becomes an existential necessity. Otherwise freedom to act at may lead to perfect libertinism and disorder in social and human relationship. She is torn between love and hate, liking and disliking for her own husband an life situations. Such a creature is the least entitled for the right of free action. She must follow rules and customs and should continue as an obedient and submissive wife.

The novelist Shashi Deshpande has chosen a humanistic bye–line, a psychological solution to Jaya's problems. She is allowed indulgence in her own egotistical feelings. The smoldering fire of suppressed feelings, the maintenance of self – control the pursuit of mechanical role of mother and son, the need to cater to the physical and emotional needs of husband and children must remain suspended for a while , or be forgotten and her real feminine soul, her pent up sufferings and feelings must find an outlet. The lid of self – control must be opened and left open for a while to allow the smoldering feelings an outlet.

Deshpande focuses on male – female rivalry as felt by Jaya. The egocentric vein in her temperament does not strive for the total fusion of identity with Mohan; she keeps intact a little bit of her own identity, her own individuality. as a married lady she become dependent on Mohan and this she considers derogatory and she feels she is reduced to " stereo type of a women; nervous ,incompetent needing male help and support" (77). In married life she wishes to maintain self- identity. Her desire for self – knowledge makes her realize her "awesome power over him" (82). DADA reveals humorously another strain of her character as a child and calls her a "pampered, bad – tempered only daughter" in her life.

Shashi Deshpande has made the revelation of Jaya's real nature the very core of the novel. Jaya is in conscious pursuit of self – knowledge. She is a model of patience, endurance, devotion, integrity, defiance and disobedience at the same tune. She is all along pursuing the idea of a self- identity. She finds it difficult to put together the different discordant acts of her personality. Thus the young bride Suhasini is at logger heads with the mature and seasoned Jaya who is both restrictive and destructive.

The tradition – bound docile women in Jaya is irreconcilable with the modern's individuality seeking Jaya. The loyal, loving Jaya – the devoted wife of Mohan – is reconcilable with the epicurean Jaya relishing a momentary embarrasses with Kamat. So the novelist is able to impart a complex identity to Jaya, focusing at the same time on the egoistic and the altruistic aspects of women hood.

There is no mutual love between Jaya and Mohan, because they never lead a life of real husband and wife; because they have not spoken freely, they never enjoyed the life; they never talked about romance, even Jaya says of her life. "As I thought of those days, of my feelings, and then looked at the man lying beside me, nothing stirred in me. Those emotions and responses seemed to belong to two other people, not to the two of us lying here together. (95).

By accepting social and familial roles imposed upon her she has eclipsed her own name. Jaya's conviction that communication between Mohan and herself, as man and woman as to individual entities was impossible, leads her to retreat into silence because it was so much simpler to say nothing so much less complicated. She says that it is easy for her to remained silent than to argue with Mohan. It is meaningless exercise of living together, Jaya feels that she lived together but there has been only emptiness between them.

Deshpande gives an account of horrible instances of ill treatment carried out in the life of married women. She bears all the cruel bearings of her drunkard husband without any hint of complaint. She has to support herself and her husband. She remains faithful to her husband even after his death. She has to earn for the liquor consumed by her husband. She brings up the children of her dead husband by 'the other woman'. Jeeja's story gets repeated in the acts of Rajaram, Jeeja's stepson. He beats his wife Tara, to extract some money for his liquor. With the case of Jeeja, the reader can find a faithful wife.

Jaya prepares herself physically and mentally to face her life in responsible manners as a wife and mother, like Jaya there are many women in world gripping about their fate, but they should come out of that struggles, this is the clear picture of this novel in woman's life marriage subjugates and enslaves woman and it leads her into contemplation of suffering life, but everyone has to awaken from that darkness into bright future. Hence, Marriage is considered as good example to show gender politics.

In order to analysis the life of Jaya she takes the new step. When Mohan her husband leaves her alone and does not return for several days, and then there is no words from him. Even Jaya gets many wounding from him she cannot tolerate her husband's fail so she is agitatedly waiting for him. She fells mental sick anyhow at last she realizes that a new life is waiting for her in the name of her husband realization and reconciliation. Somehow she attains what she wants in her life because she has the confidence to face problems and hopes to achieve it.

Jaya feels that life without Mohan is vague and vacant. She is very hopefully longs for the arrival of her husband.

I had to stop this I had to get a grip on myself. None of this made sense, none it was true. Mohan had not left me, he would be back. If there was nothing else to reassure me, there was my knowledge of Mohan, of the utter strength of his convictions: a husband and wife care for each other. Live with each other until they are dead; parents care for their children and children in turn look after their parents when they are needed; marriage never end, they cannot. They are a state of being. (TLS,127).

Jaya firmly believes that Mohan will come back to her and he will be repentant for his failure and job. A woman cannot get rid of marriage, because marriage never ends. She has to take life as it comes and finally she decides it is foolish to be rebellious. Revolutionary ideas in a family give sufferings and hardships. Even though she has confined herself in gender politics, she has some courage to lead her life with femininity and at last she had attained her happiness in marital space.

Deshpande's novel depicts the suffering, agony and tension of her protagonist but end with an optimistic note. She fascinated with woman character and she wants to show the freedom of women's life. Her protagonists are highly sensitive, intelligent and educated. Jaya is compared with Ammu, a character is Arunthathi Roy's *God of Small Things.* Ammu is a victim of circumstances, where as Jaya is the modern educated enlightened woman in search of the fulfillment of the self. Several writers make conscious attempts to analyse the predicaments of woman from various angles. Deshpande is one such novelist who provides searching insights and great deal of human understanding.

That Long Silence is to break the silence; it is a real thrust on women's freedom and exhibits their position in society by the domineering males. In almost of her writings, Shashi Deshpande tries to project the fact that tales about women, which is so far had been narrated from man's point of view, should be retold from woman's point of view. They will have go fight their own battles, nobody is going to do it for them. Deshpande is primarily concerned with the woman and her eternal quest for life.

G. Lakshmi Narasaiah cleverly discovers the existential theme in Shashi Deshpande's novel. According to the critic: "Jaya speaks not like women liberated from the burdens of either her humanity or her womanhood, but a woman redefining her existential situation I her own terms, having it out 'on her own premises." (136)

Jaya and Mohan's life of marriage reminds one of Anita Desai'snovels *Cry thePeacock* where an ever widening gap in communication between Maya and her husband is felt throughout the novel. In Shashi Deshpande's novel *That Long Silence* Jaya's mournful silence and the painful sufferings leave her into emotional disturbance and mental suppression but the novel ends with an affirmative note.

Undoubtedly, tolerance, love, kindness and faithfulness are widely acknowledged traits of female nature or called in the name of feminine qualities, but self-assertion is not to be viewed as contrary to these values. It is on this point that the feminist in Shashi Deshpande steps in. She presents a woman's picture of female with exact traditional femininities. She brings to surface the protesting and defiant aspect of their character, the contexts, figures and situations are mythological but the responses and reactions of her protagonist's are similar to those of contemporary women. The characters are portrayed as reactionary.

The recent of women has undergone a giant hike in the recent decades. Education gives new exposure to women in the fast growing world. Urbanization is increasing number of career for women. Consciousness of their own strength and status in society are some of the reasons for emancipation of women. The changing the status of women has revolutionized the system of family and literature too. This theme of self realization has become a major theme to literary artists, theorists, and sociologists. Though we have overcome many evil practices like child marriage and sati, the image of Sita and Savithri is still there in the mind of Indian community, this in essence is the theme of Deshpande's works. The conflict between the light of education and exposure and the darkness of the old tradition and the values is the essence of her novels.

Deshpande clearly stems from her roots of writing, explained in day today India. Her major concerns emerge from our own environment, from our immediate world, holding up mirrors to our own lives. Her works are gender specific and involved in gender politics. As a woman is unable to expose their desires, even nobody is ready to ask her wishes. So she feels insecurity in her life and she is always pushed into the dark room. Therefore through her writings, Shashi Deshpande portrays the inner turmoil of woman, fighting within herself, to come out of the chaos.

Deshpande's heroines emerge from a conservative, middle class, semi-urban milieu. While it gives them an inherent strength to survive, it also handicaps them by burdening them with heavy inhibitions. Her writing career makes her to create her own world. And also it allows her a safe place from which she can explore a wide range of experience, especially in regard to woman's status in society.

In the Indian society men never treat their wives as a companion but as submissive and subordinate figure. Basically she writes about the situation of women and their failures in the fast changing world. Her writing comes out of her consciousness of the conflict between her idea of herself as a human being and the idea that society has of her as a woman. Her heroines inspire of their conflict with traditions, wish to live for her family framework relationship, with great intelligent. She employs her writings as a vehicle to probe into women's lives and experiences. She is deeply concerned with freedom of women in her novels to make them aware of themselves and their individuality.

Women writers probe into human relationships, since the present problem is concerned with mind and heart. The English exposed Indian to western life styles, modes of thinking and attitudes. *That Long Silence* represents a silence of Indian women's life with its ups and downs because of the gender politics. It depicts the realistic dramatization of the married life of women. Like Jaya many women are in the world accepting about their fate, but it should not continue in their life, they could come out of their struggles. For that thirst Shashi Deshpande writes her novels. Actually she exploits in her work what she sees around her atmosphere.

In these novels Deshpande raises her strong voice of protest against the male domination and gender discrimination. Jaya doesn't feel happy about her life; she is always in the mood of basing her individually because there is no status of self in her life. She has to live always for other. *That Long Silence* is a typical Indian English novel, speaks to each and every ideal woman and explains their situation. Deshpande being a woman writer wants to expose her views and ideas of the society.

Deshpande's humanism acquires cultural and also spiritual overtones. Her interest in writing of women and their state in Indian society and large traditional joint families, superiority of male children and men in Indian families arouse a mild sense of anger and feminist anger in most of her novels. She balances her opines of women as victims of male apathy or cruelty.

Sarala Parker beautifully sums up the idea and she says: "the important insight that Deshpande imparts to us through Jaya have contributed to their victimization instead of putting the blame on everybody except themselves." (86)

That Long Silence reveals the sincerity and ability in voicing the concerns of the urban educated middle-class. She desires and shows keen interest in the empowerment of women in the multifaceted aspects of life.The woman of Shashi Deshpande's novels faces formidable challenges to gain their right place in the society. The major problems faced by her women characters are the psychological discrimination. Women are considered to be the weaker sex, but one can see glimpses of women with great power of endurance, affinity, love and foresight contributing to the happiness of others. Every woman possess all power and femininity to product her marital life.

Through this simple story of Jaya, Deshpande has raised many issues related to matrimony, and questioned the concepts of love and marriage. This is what S.P. swain means when he says: "A sensitive and realistic dramatization of the married life of Jaya and her husband Mohan, it [that long silence] portrays an inquisitive critical appraisal to which the institution of marriage has been subjected to in recent years." (87)

Deshpande is one of the ranking Indian women novelists in English who has written interesting novels on contemporary themes. Indian house wife maintains her silence in the face of untold agonies of life. Normally woman has strength to tolerate her life for others. The family is under the shed of the woman, patience, tolerance, acceptance and adjustments, the four important sources, with which woman makes her family prosperous and successful. Woman is symbol of sacrifice. Never in a moment she lives for herself, is she considered avatharam to help other? In *Roots and Shadows*, Mini and Akka sacrifices their life for others.

Deshpande generally has the heroine as the narrator, and employs a stream-of-consciousness method of narration. The narrative goes back and forth, so the narrator can describe events with the benefit of retrospection. It would not be correct to call her a feminist, because there is nothing doctrinaire about her fiction; she simply portrays, in depth, the meaning of being a woman in modern India.

Deshpande felt that she was consciously translating Indian culture into English. It was only after writing her third one that she became more at ease. Deshpande gives in her work about the psychology of women. Though she is wife, mother or daughter-in-law she has to obey and to under the guidance of man realistically and credibly. She presents a middle class, suffering and sobbing and silent feminine woman. Gender politics is prevailing in society and experienced by woman than men. Deshpande is so much fascinated with woman character and she wants to show the freedom of women's life.

That Long Silence tells the story of Jaya and the novel expands through various stages of her physical, mental and emotional developments. As every other Indian girl had been born and trained according to the conventional practices of the Indian society. The Indian girlhood was a well protected one and their father was very fond of love with girl child particularly in this novel. He gave her much freedom with an insight that she was not an ordinary girl. Because of this influence, she failed to find friends in her schools and colleges. After the death of her father, Jaya was always terribly alone. But she could never complain of her loneliness.

Sumitra Kukreti remarks, "the realization that she [Jaya] can have her own way – yathecchasi tatha kuru – gives a new confidence to Jaya. This is her emancipation." (87) In *That Long Silence* she makes an aesthetic plea to free the female psyche from the clutch of conventional male domineering society. In short, almost all the literary ventures of Shashi Deshpande revolve around the pathetic and heart rendering condition of women in a male dominated society. For this, she never suggests female domination as a solution to it. She points out the importance of self realization among Indian women. She believes that all the path breaking discoveries are the outcome of our faith, which helps mankind like a ladder to reach the Zenith. For the very beginning of the novel, *That Long Silence*, she stresses this.

The theme of cultural conflict or reconciliation assumes a pivotal place in the recent fiction by Indian writers. It is more than a manifestation of the Indian writer's constant awareness of the changing traditions. Further, the process of realizing herself creatively in the English exposes her to western culture. The protagonist's awareness of these two civilizations exhilarates their search for their own identity. They are all in search of their true image, tossing between the traditional values they have absorbed from childhood and the new values have absorbed by their education and their association with the west has bestowed open them.

Jaya emerges as an individual within a distinct identify, as Indra Mohan writes: "She [jaya] breaks herself-imposed prison wall of mind and chooses to remain I the family at the same time comes out of the confining slots allotted to her by the patriarchal society." (117).

Most of the women employ a mode of social realism. History rarely gives space to women and get it is women who keep history alive by carrying on the burden of the past and samskaras. The institution of marriage, eulogized by male, has been viewed by women writers as something debilitating, restricting and emotionally fragmenting for the female protagonist. Shashi Deshpande's *That Long Silence* has a slight resemblance to Henrik Ibsen's *A Doll's house* both Ibsen and Deshpande could draw the attention of readers on these works and both wrote their works with a sense of social commitments and exhibit gender politics of the society. So these works have a social relevance also. Both the works unveil the true condition of women on those particular periods. Feminism leaning of marriage, theme of isolation, the quest for identity, self realization etc., are the major themes shared in these works. Both reflect the nature of themes with their titles also.

Women's double marginalization through patriarchy and imperialistic ideologies is a dominant point of reflection and discussions in all fictional works of women writers. In a middle class family, man tries to convince his family that he is the spine of the family which keeps standing it erect. *That Long Silence* handles this kind of marginalization and minimizing role of women in their family. Jaya's husband Mohan was this sort of a person and he cleverly veils his guilt by his repeated appraisal that he was a dutiful son and he is a dutiful father, husband, brother. But Mohan's statement breaks Jaya by his description of her nuptial life.

Our women writers have succeeded in writing about the real problems of Indian women and their lives inside the four walls of their house. The life of Indian women is different when compare to the women of other nations. Our country is famous for educated and successful people but there is an old stock of traditional norms, which pulls back the social betterment of Indian female community such as the identity of women being incomplete, if lacking the name of their husbands or fathers along with their names. And it is also believed that women have no independent existence even if she is educated or employed. Our women writers have graphically depicted this narrow – mindedness in many novels and other literary forms.

The Indian woman has for years been a silent sufferer. While she has played different roles-as a wife, mother, sister and daughter, she has never been able to claim her own individuality. The words which we always associate with what we consider to be the concept of an ideal woman or feminine women are self-denial, sacrifice, patience, devotion and silent suffering always. A woman was and is expected to subordinate one, each and every wish and desire is decided by someone else a parent, a husband or a child.

That Long Silence, the women protagonists in these novels achieve "personhood" yet do not counteract the family or the society. They go beyond what Elaine Showalter calls the "Female phase" which is a phase of self-discovery, a turning inward freed from the dependence of opposition, a search for identity".They do doubt to discover them but the quest does not end there.*That Long Silence* is about a writer going through an anxious breakdown while her marriage seems poised to dissolve. 'Deshpande's novels are not about pleasure' this statement is given by Rushdie. Her writing style is too fit her themes. She is adept at evoking the claustrophobic world of her protagonists without too many stylistic fireworks. In many ways she goes against the grain of what Indian writers in English are usually thought to be "like" or "about".

Deshpande's novels present a social world of many complex relationships. Like the densely carved architecture of Indian temples there are, in Deshpande's works, many men and women living together, traveling around across life in their different age groups, classes and gendered roles. *Roots and Shadows* projects the educated women who are unable to adapt the traditional feminine background in which they are reared.

Deshpande wants to transform the society and she realises the inevitability for women's education and economic independence which can eradicate deficiency. She is concerned with the duties of a devoted wife 'pathivrata' and with these women's inner struggle to revolt against slavery. But her women come to the point of compromise and avoid all open fights. They practice non-violence and advocate that people should learn to negotiate disagreements and problems without fighting. This is seen at the end of *That Long Silence* where the women protagonist, Jaya decides to clarify the matter with her husband.

Parker says Deshpande seems to give the message that **"women should accept their own responsibility for what they are, see how much they have contributed to their own victimization…, It is only through self-analysis and self – understanding, through vigilance and courage, they can begin to change their lives." (158)**

Deshpande has dealt graphically with the problems deal with middle-class educated women in the patriarchal Hindu society. Deshpande's heroine is not like the women of Anita Desai, neurotic and hysterical. She is not a Maya or a Monisha ever ready to face the "ferocious assaults of existence" (Desai interviewed, Times of India, 1979).

Marriage subjugates and enslaves woman. It leads her to "aimless days indefinitely repeated, life that slips away gently toward death without questioning its purpose" (De Beauvoir 1974: 500). Women pay for their happiness at the cost of their freedom. De Beauvoir emphasized that such a sacrifice on the part of a woman is too high for anyone since the kind of self-contentment and security that marriage offers woman drains her soul of its capacity for great

Indian tradition considers the marriage ceremony as one in which the husband and wife become one however that one is the husband. In an Indian marriage it is understood that the wife will merge her name-personality, life style and intact, her entire life that of the husband. Initially Deshande wants to change the society. The predominating issues and terms in her novels arise from the situations that focus on women caught. In the crisis of a transitional society where the shift is taking place from traditional to modern. The novelist paint to notice ways of subordinating women by male members of the society.

Every Indian woman improved a lot to get out of her struggles and sufferings with their hope. Likewise Shashi's novels end up with the women who are facing the problems with courage and valor. In comparison with Anita Desai's characters they are oversensitive characters. They find solution for their weakness committing suicide, in Nayantara Sahgal, other contemporaries of Shashi Deshpande shows her female characters defy the traditional norms in search of emancipation.

Deshpande shows her characters', especially the women facing their problems bravely at last they find a positive solution. They all realised the importance of their family, this makes them lead their life in correct formation, the affirmation rather than rejection. Her women characters find their rightful place in the society.

Jaya comes to the point of compromise and avoids all open fights. She practices non-violence and advocates that she has to negotiate disagreement and problems without fight. It may be observed that the exigencies of life presented themselves in the form of traumatic events to Jaya. Her psyche has not been well-equipped to meet them. As a result the floodgates of anxiety have been suddenly opened and at this psychological moment irrationality qualified her response to the situation. However, soon she has mustered up enough inner strength to state a return to normalcy. The experience has provided her with an ideal occasion for growing introspective and thus make important discovery about her and redefine her relation with the world.

Jaya's experience is universal. It indicates that many women are troubled by the fact that they do have no choices. The route of their crisis suggested is that they stop focusing on missed opportunities and take up those still on offer. By turning protested, by resisting, Jaya translates her feeling of inadequacy into a better idea of what she wants. Deshpande's characters find freedom not in the western sense but in conformity with the society they live in without drifting away from one's culture. Jaya's decision is not meek surrender to circumstances, but a sensible compromise. Deshpande supports the view that feminism is pro-woman but not anti-man; she rejects a separatist stance. Aware of the fact that breaking off the bonds of family would results in loneliness and disintegration of the larger social set up, Jaya looks for happiness and fulfillment within the family itself.

Deshpande wants to transform the society and she realizes the inevitability of women's right place in the society. She emphasis the importance of acceptability and also enunciate the change is the only thing that never changes. She emphasis the real truth nonviolence is powerful than any other thing in the world. At the final the two protagonists were handled their temperance in right way to attain their real success. Everyone should rectify the problem without fight and hostility; this is seen at the end of the novel in *That Long Silence* when the woman protagonist, Jaya decides to clarify the matter with her husband, on his return from his self-imposed exile. At last she brings out and enables them to move in positive direction.

Deshpande stresses that by writing like a woman is to explore the range of one's own sensibility without the influence of any narrow masculine pattern, and to feel entirely confident in one's own judgment and value. Usually Female authors indulge themselves in over rapture of female characters and exhibit liking towards them by foregrounding the strengths of their female characters over their weaknesses; and reveal deterioration of male counterparts. Likewise male writers are intrinsically inclined towards male characters and replicate patriarchy in their works. It has also been examined that indisputable representation of men by women writers and women by men authors, is not possible; there is always writer's gender bias involved in the depiction of characters that was exactly proved in the writings of Shashi Deshpande. Gender characteristics and gendered depiction are the central concerns in this anal and concludes that gender definitely apart from natural sex but it plays a very important role in determining male and female characterization in literature.

Keywords:

TLS: THAT LONG Silence , Deshpande: Sashi Deshpande.

THREE
CONCLUSION

Deshpande clearly stems from her roots of writing, explained in day today India. Her major concerns emerge from our own environment, from our immediate world, holding up mirrors to our own lives. Her works are gender specific and involved in gender politics. As a woman is unable to expose their desires, even nobody is ready to ask her wishes. So she feels insecurity in her life and she is always pushed into the dark room. Therefore through her writings, Shashi Deshpande portrays the inner turmoil of woman, fighting within herself, to come out of the chaos.

Deshpande's heroines emerge from a conservative, middle class, semi-urban milieu. While it gives them an inherent strength to survive, it also handicaps them by burdening them with heavy inhibitions. Her writing career makes her to create her own world. And also it allows her a safe place from which she can explore a wide range of experience, especially in regard to woman's status in society.

In the Indian society men never treat their wives as a companion but as submissive and subordinate figure. Basically she writes about the situation of women and their failures in the fast changing world. Her writing comes out of her consciousness of the conflict between her idea of herself as a human being and the idea that society has of her as a woman. Her heroines inspire of their conflict with traditions, wish to live for her family framework relationship, with great intelligent. She employs her writings as a vehicle to probe into women's lives and experiences. She is deeply concerned with freedom of women in her novels to make them aware of themselves and their individuality.

Women writers probe into human relationships, since the present problem is concerned with mind and heart. The English exposed Indian to western life styles, modes of thinking and attitudes. *That Long Silence* represents a silence of Indian women's life with its ups and downs because of the gender politics. It depicts the realistic dramatization of the married life of women. Like Jaya many women are in the world accepting about their fate, but it should not continue in their life, they could come out of their struggles. For that thirst Shashi Deshpande writes her novels. Actually she exploits in her work what she sees around her atmosphere.

In these novels Deshpande raises her strong voice of protest against the male domination and gender discrimination. Jaya doesn't feel happy about her life; she is always in the mood of basing her individually because there is no status of self in her life. She has to live always for other. *That Long Silence* is a typical Indian English novel, speaks to each and every ideal woman and explains their situation. Deshpande being a woman writer wants to expose her views and ideas of the society.

Deshpande's humanism acquires cultural and also spiritual overtones. Her interest in writing of women and their state in Indian society and large traditional joint families, superiority of male children and men in Indian families arouse a mild sense of anger and feminist anger in most of her novels. She balances her opines of women as victims of male apathy or cruelty.

Sarala Parker beautifully sums up the idea and she says: "the important insight that Deshpande imparts to us through Jaya have contributed to their victimization instead of putting the blame on everybody except themselves." (86) *That Long Silence* reveals the sincerity and ability in voicing the concerns of the urban educated middle-class. She desires and shows keen interest in the empowerment of women in the multifaceted aspects of life.The woman of Shashi Deshpande's novels faces formidable challenges to gain their right place in the society. The major problems faced by her women characters are the psychological discrimination. Women are considered to be the weaker sex, but one can see glimpses of women with great power of endurance, affinity, love and foresight contributing to the happiness of others. Every woman possess all power and femininity to product her marital life.

Through this simple story of Jaya, Deshpande has raised many issues related to matrimony, and questioned the concepts of love and marriage. This is what S.P. swain means when he says: "A sensitive and realistic dramatization of the married life of Jaya and her husband Mohan, it [that long silence] portrays an inquisitive critical appraisal to which the institution of marriage has been subjected to in recent years." (87)

Deshpande is one of the ranking Indian women novelists in English who has written interesting novels on contemporary themes. Indian house wife maintains her silence in the face of untold agonies of life. Normally woman has strength to tolerate her life for others. The family is under the shed of the woman, patience, tolerance, acceptance and adjustments, the four important sources, with which woman makes her family prosperous and successful. Woman is symbol of sacrifice. Never in a moment she lives for herself, is she considered avatharam to help other? In *Roots and Shadows*, Mini and Akka sacrifices their life for others.

Deshpande generally has the heroine as the narrator, and employs a stream-of-consciousness method of narration. The narrative goes back and forth, so the narrator can describe events with the benefit of retrospection. It would not be correct to call her a feminist, because there is nothing doctrinaire about her fiction; she simply portrays, in depth, the meaning of being a woman in modern India.

Deshpande felt that she was consciously translating Indian culture into English. It was only after writing her third one that she became more at ease. Deshpande gives in her work about the psychology of women. Though she is wife, mother or daughter-in-law she has to obey and to under the guidance of man realistically and credibly. She presents a middle class, suffering and sobbing and silent feminine woman. Gender politics is prevailing in society and experienced by woman than men. Deshpande is so much fascinated with woman character and she wants to show the freedom of women's life.

That Long Silence tells the story of Jaya and the novel expands through various stages of her physical, mental and emotional developments. As every other Indian girl had been born and trained according to the conventional practices of the Indian society. The Indian girlhood was a well protected one and their father was very fond of love with girl child particularly in this novel. He gave her much freedom with an insight that she was not an ordinary girl. Because of this influence, she failed to find friends in her schools and colleges. After the death of her father, Jaya was always terribly alone. But she could never complain of her loneliness.

Sumitra Kukreti remarks, "the realization that she [Jaya] can have her own way – yathecchasi tatha kuru – gives a new confidence to Jaya. This is her emancipation." (87) In *That Long Silence* she makes an aesthetic plea to free the female psyche from the clutch of conventional male domineering society. In short, almost all the literary ventures of Shashi Deshpande revolve around the pathetic and heart rendering condition of women in a male dominated society. For this, she never suggests female domination as a solution to it. She points out the importance of self realization among Indian women. She believes that all the path breaking discoveries are the outcome of our faith, which helps mankind like a ladder to reach the Zenith. For the very beginning of the novel, *That Long Silence*, she stresses this.

The theme of cultural conflict or reconciliation assumes a pivotal place in the recent fiction by Indian writers. It is more than a manifestation of the Indian writer's constant awareness of the changing traditions. Further, the process of realizing herself creatively in the English exposes her to western culture. The protagonist's awareness of these two civilizations exhilarates their search for their own identity. They are all in search of their true image, tossing between the traditional values they have absorbed from childhood and the new values have absorbed by their education and their association with the west has bestowed open them.

Jaya emerges as an individual within a distinct identify, as Indra Mohan writes: "She [jaya] breaks herself-imposed prison wall of mind and chooses to remain I the family at the same time comes out of the confining slots allotted to her by the patriarchal society." (117).

Most of the women employ a mode of social realism. History rarely gives space to women and get it is women who keep history alive by carrying on the burden of the past and samskaras. The institution of marriage, eulogized by male, has been viewed by women writers as something debilitating, restricting and emotionally fragmenting for the female protagonist. Shashi Deshpande's *That Long Silence* has a slight resemblance to Henrik Ibsen's *A Doll's house* both Ibsen and Deshpande could draw the attention of readers on these works and both wrote their works with a sense of social commitments and exhibit gender politics of the society. So these works have a social relevance also. Both the works unveil the true condition of women on those particular periods. Feminism leaning of marriage, theme of isolation, the quest for identity, self realization etc., are the major themes shared in these works. Both reflect the nature of themes with their titles also.

Women's double marginalization through patriarchy and imperialistic ideologies is a dominant point of reflection and discussions in all fictional works of women writers. In a middle class family, man tries to convince his family that he is the spine of the family which keeps standing it erect. *That Long Silence* handles this kind of marginalization and minimizing role of women in their family. Jaya's husband Mohan was this sort of a person and he cleverly veils his guilt by his repeated appraisal that he was a dutiful son and he is a dutiful father, husband, brother. But Mohan's statement breaks Jaya by his description of her nuptial life.

Our women writers have succeeded in writing about the real problems of Indian women and their lives inside the four walls of their house. The life of Indian women is different when compare to the women of other nations. Our country is famous for educated and successful people but there is an old stock of traditional norms, which pulls back the social betterment of Indian female community such as the identity of women being incomplete, if lacking the name of their husbands or fathers along with their names. And it is also believed that women have no independent existence even if she is educated or employed. Our women writers have graphically depicted this narrow – mindedness in many novels and other literary forms.

The Indian woman has for years been a silent sufferer. While she has played different roles-as a wife, mother, sister and daughter, she has never been able to claim her own individuality. The words which we always associate with what we consider to be the concept of an ideal woman or feminine women are self-denial, sacrifice, patience, devotion and silent suffering always. A woman was and is expected to subordinate one, each and every wish and desire is decided by someone else a parent, a husband or a child.

That Long Silence, the women protagonists in these novels achieve "personhood" yet do not counteract the family or the society. They go beyond what Elaine Showalter calls the "Female phase" which is a phase of self-discovery, a turning inward freed from the dependence of opposition, a search for identity".They do doubt to discover them but the quest does not end there.*That Long Silence* is about a writer going through an anxious breakdown while her marriage seems poised to dissolve. 'Deshpande's novels are not about pleasure' this statement is given by Rushdie. Her writing style is too fit her themes. She is adept at evoking the claustrophobic world of her protagonists without too many stylistic fireworks. In many ways she goes against the grain of what Indian writers in English are usually thought to be "like" or "about".

Deshpande's novels present a social world of many complex relationships. Like the densely carved architecture of Indian temples there are, in Deshpande's works, many men and women living together, traveling around across life in their different age groups, classes and gendered roles. *Roots and Shadows* projects the educated women who are unable to adapt the traditional feminine background in which they are reared.

Deshpande wants to transform the society and she realises the inevitability for women's education and economic independence which can eradicate deficiency. She is concerned with the duties of a devoted wife 'pathivrata' and with these women's inner struggle to revolt against slavery. But her women come to the point of compromise and avoid all open fights. They practice non-violence and advocate that people should learn to negotiate disagreements and problems without fighting. This is seen at the end of *That Long Silence* where the women protagonist, Jaya decides to clarify the matter with her husband.

Parker says Deshpande seems to give the message that **"women should accept their own responsibility for what they are, see how much they have contributed to their own victimization..., It is only through self-analysis and self – understanding, through vigilance and courage, they can begin to change their lives." (158)**

Deshpande has dealt graphically with the problems deal with middle-class educated women in the patriarchal Hindu society. Deshpande's heroine is not like the women of Anita Desai, neurotic and hysterical. She is not a Maya or a Monisha ever ready to face the "ferocious assaults of existence" (Desai interviewed, Times of India, 1979).

Marriage subjugates and enslaves woman. It leads her to "aimless days indefinitely repeated, life that slips away gently toward death without questioning its purpose" (De Beauvoir 1974: 500). Women pay for their happiness at the cost of their freedom. De Beauvoir emphasized that such a sacrifice on the part of a woman is too high for anyone since the kind of self-contentment and security that marriage offers woman drains her soul of its capacity for greatness.

Indian tradition considers the marriage ceremony as one in which the husband and wife become one however that one is the husband. In an Indian marriage it is understood that the wife will merge her name-personality, life style and intact, her entire life that of the husband. Initially Deshande wants to change the society. The predominating issues and terms in her novels arise from the situations that focus on women caught. In the crisis of a transitional society where the shift is taking place from traditional to modern. The novelist paint to notice ways of subordinating women by male members of the society.

Every Indian woman improved a lot to get out of her struggles and sufferings with their hope. Likewise Shashi's novels end up with the women who are facing the problems with courage and valor. In comparison with Anita Desai's characters they are oversensitive characters. They find solution for their weakness committing suicide, in Nayantara Sahgal, other contemporaries of Shashi Deshpande shows her female characters defy the traditional norms in search of emancipation.

Deshpande shows her characters', especially the women facing their problems bravely at last they find a positive solution. They all realised the importance of their family, this makes them lead their life in correct formation, the affirmation rather than rejection. Her women characters find their rightful place in the society.

Jaya comes to the point of compromise and avoids all open fights. She practices non-violence and advocates that she has to negotiate disagreement and problems without fight. It may be observed that the exigencies of life presented themselves in the form of traumatic events to Jaya. Her psyche has not been well-equipped to meet them. As a result the floodgates of anxiety have been suddenly opened and at this psychological moment irrationality qualified her response to the situation. However, soon she has mustered up enough inner strength to state a return to normalcy. The experience has provided her with an ideal occasion for growing introspective and thus make important discovery about her and redefine her relation with the world.

Jaya's experience is universal. It indicates that many women are troubled by the fact that they do have no choices. The route of their crisis suggested is that they stop focusing on missed opportunities and take up those still on offer. By turning protested, by resisting, Jaya translates her feeling of inadequacy into a better idea of what she wants. Deshpande's characters find freedom not in the western sense but in conformity with the society they live in without drifting away from one's culture. Jaya's decision is not meek surrender to circumstances, but a sensible compromise. Deshpande supports the view that feminism is pro-woman but not anti-man; she rejects a separatist stance. Aware of the fact that breaking off the bonds of family would results in loneliness and disintegration of the larger social set up, Jaya looks for happiness and fulfillment within the family itself.

Deshpande wants to transform the society and she realizes the inevitability of women's right place in the society. She emphasis the importance of acceptability and also enunciate the change is the only thing that never changes. She emphasis the real truth nonviolence is powerful than any other thing in the world. At the final the two protagonists were handled their temperance in right way to attain their real success. Everyone should rectify the problem without fight and hostility; this is seen at the end of the novel in *That Long Silence* when the woman protagonist, Jaya decides to clarify the matter with her husband, on his return from his self-imposed exile. At last she brings out and enables them to move in positive direction.

Deshpande stresses that by writing like a woman is to explore the range of one's own sensibility without the influence of any narrow masculine pattern, and to feel entirely confident in one's own judgment and value. Usually Female authors indulge themselves in over rapture of female characters and exhibit liking towards them by foregrounding the strengths of their female characters over their weaknesses; and reveal deterioration of male counterparts. Likewise male writers are intrinsically inclined towards male characters and replicate patriarchy in their works. It has also been examined that indisputable representation of men by women writers and women by men authors, is not possible; there is always writer's gender bias involved in the depiction of characters that was exactly proved in the writings of Shashi Deshpande. Gender characteristics and gendered depiction are the central concerns in this anal and concludes that gender definitely apart from natural sex but it plays a very important role in determining male and female characterization in literature.

Work Cited

Deshpande, Shashi. *That Long Silence*, (New Delhi : Penguin, 1989). Print.

..., *Roots and shadows*. Delhi: Viking, 2000. Print.

Ahuja Suman, The Times of India. 8th October 1989, P.2. Print.

Das Kumar Bijay, *Post-Modern Indian English Literature* (New Delhi: Atlantic publishers and Distributors, 2003), pp.81-82. Print.

Dinesh Kamini, *"Moving out of the Cloistered self : Deshpane's protagonists." Margins of Erasure : Purdah in the Subcontinental Novel in English.* Ed.Jashbir Jain and Amma Amin. New Delhi : Sterling,1995.P.196. Print.

Dwivedi, A.An. "Shashi Deshpande's *That long Silence:* a Feminist Reading," Writing the Female : Akademi Awarded Novels in English in English, ed. Mithilesh K. Pandey (New Delhi: Sarup and Sons, 2004). P.88 Print.

Gaur Rashmi, *"Images of Indian Woman in Shashi Deshpande's That Long Silence-stereotypes, Myths and Realities"* in writing the female: Akademi Awarded Novels in English. Methilesh K.Panday New Delhi : Sarup & Sons, 2004. P-179. Print.

Kukrerti Sumitra, qt. in S. Prasanna Sree, *Women in the Novels of Shashi Deshpande* : A study, P. 87. Print.

Lakshmi Narasaiah, G. *"Life inside the Cage*: Shashi Deshpande,s *"That long Silance"*, "The Indian Novel with a Social purpose, ed. K. Venkata Reddy and P. Bayapa Reddy (New Delhi: Atlantic Publishers and Distribters, 1999), P. 136. Print.

Mohan Indra T.M.J., *"Feminist perspectives in Shashi Deshpande,s "That Long Silence and The Dark Holds No Terrrors,"* Shashi Deshpande: a critical spectrum, P. 117. Print.

Parker Sarala, qt. in S. Prasanna Sree, *Woman in the Novels of Shashi Deshpande*: A Study (New Delhi: Sarup and Sons, 2003), P.86. Print.

Parker Sarla, qt. in Pashupati Jha and Nagendra kumar, *"Looking Back in Anger*: Shashi Deshpande,s That long Silance,"

WORK CITED

Writing the Female : Akademi Awarded Novel in English, ed. Mithilesh K. Pandey, P.158. Print.

Rajan Rajeswari Sunder, *"The Feminist plot and the Nationalist Allegory*: Home and world in Two Indian Women's Novels in English". Modern Fiction Studies.39.1 (Spring 1993) pp.876-88. Print.

Sandhu Sarabjit, *The image of Women in the novels of Shashi Deshpande* (New Dlhi: Prestige Books, 1991), P. 40. Print.

Sethuraman, N. *"Silence, Surrender and Compromise* : A study of Shashi Deshpande's That Long Silence" "Shashi Deshpande" A Critical Spectrum, ed, T.M.J Indira Mohan, P.194. Print.

Sinha Urvashi and Gur Pyar Jandial , " *Marriage and sexually in the Novels of Shashi Deshpande,"* Shashi Deshpande : A Critical spectrum, P. 130. Print.

Swain S.P., "Feminism in Shashi Deshpande's Novels." *Contemporary Indian Writing in English* : Critical Perceptions. New Delhi : Sarup @ Son, 205. P.125. Print.

..., "Articulation of the Feminine Vice: Jaya in Shashi Deshpande's *That Long Silence,"* Shashi Deshpande : *A Critical spectrum,* ed. T.M.J. Indra Mohan (New Delhi : Atlantic Publishers and Distributors, 2004), P.87. Print.

..., "Feminism in Shashi Deshpande's Novels," *Contemporary Indian Writing in English*: critical Perceptions, ed. N.D.R. Chandra, II (New Delhi: Sarup and Sons, 2005), P.129. Print.